MW01193717

Printed in the United States of America
ISBN: 978-0-557-05367-4

Edited by Robin Crawford
Cover Design and Layout: Brandon Walker
All Photographs: Brandon Jennings; www.brandonpicts.com

Dedicated to Dr. Ira H. Peak, Jr.
My uncle and one of the most inspiring
people I've ever known.

INERTIA

"Seven Principles of Leadership in Motion"

By Brandon Walker

"**Every body continues in its state of rest, or of uniform motion in a right line, unless it is compelled to change that state by forces impressed upon it.**"

– Sir Isaac Newton

At this moment there is a man-made object nine billion miles from here hurtling through space at approximately thirty-eight thousand miles an hour. On September 5, 1977, N.A.S.A. launched the *Voyager I* space probe to travel to and report scientific data from the gas planets of Jupiter, Saturn, Uranus, and Neptune. In April of 2007, *Voyager I* entered the "heliosheath" and officially left our solar system. Although the probe was fitted with a fantastic array of cameras, recorders, and a variety of sensory equipment, it has no propulsion systems of its own. It continues to fly through space because of the initial energy applied to it when it left the earth's atmosphere at launch. While it does have on-board power sources used to run its computers and to adjust its orientation so that its instruments face the earth, the energy that is causing it to move is the same energy that flung it from the earth's atmosphere in 1977. The spacecraft will continue to travel through space at a constant speed until it eventually collides with another object or disintegrates over time. Theoretically, *Voyager I* could float through the universe for hundreds, thousands, or millions of years before it ceases to exist. Objects in motion tend to stay in motion.

In 6th grade I failed reading class. I remember the disbelief in my mother's voice as she looked over my report card, "A, A, A... D?!" I had been reading since I was four, so there was no obvious reason why I would be failing reading class. If the class were only about reading, I would have been making an easy "A" at that point, but in sixth grade, there was more to reading class than knowing how to read. In my class, students were required to stand up in front of the group and deliver a brief oral report on a book they had recently read. We were expected to do this every three weeks or so. On the day of the oral reports, I sat sweating and hunched in my chair, praying fervently that Mr. Blankenship would somehow forget to call my name. When he did eventually ask me to stand up and give my report to the class, I quietly responded that I had forgotten to read a book and thus had no report to give. Mr. Blankenship looked at me with a classic "disappointed" look and called the next student on the list. Every three weeks when oral report time came, I concocted a new and progressively more creative excuse as to why I was unable to present mine to the group. I failed the reading class not because I couldn't read, but because I simply refused to stand up in front of the class and do *anything*. I was completely paralyzed by shyness. Objects at rest tend to stay at rest.

The concept of inertia is fairly straightforward: If an object is not moving, it will remain still until an outside force causes it to move. Once that object moves, it will continue to move in a straight line until something stops it or causes it to change direction. This simple idea is also one of the keys to understanding leadership. A leader is someone who influences an object at rest, a person in a sedentary state, and causes them to move forward. If that person is already moving forward, a leader can influence that person in such a way that they change direction. Leadership is essentially the act of causing a person, or people, to *move*. Let's take a brief look at the word "move." When a person says something like, "That song really moves me," what exactly are they saying? Although the music may inspire them to move physically, what they are referring to is the music's ability to stir them emotionally, to cause something to happen in their mind, their soul. The song causes them to feel a certain way, to have certain thoughts and emotions which, in turn, cause them to act a certain way in response. This is the call of a leader... to influence, to create response.

In the advertising business, people often refer to an advertisement's "call to action." You can see this concept illustrated over and over if you happen to watch late-night TV. When you see an infomercial for some amazing new product late at night, you almost always see a call to action: "Call now! Operators are standing by!" Last night I saw an ad for some random, ridiculous product (I think it was a blanket with sleeves) that actually had a countdown clock counting down the seconds remaining in the "one time offer." The implication was that if I did not respond to the commercial in an expedient fashion, I would miss the opportunity of purchasing the very necessary product at an "unbelievably low price." The whole point of advertising is to cause consumers to feel emotions which will then cause them to purchase a particular product. Were I in dire need of the advertised product on the infomercial, I might have felt a sense of loss or disappointment that I had not called when I had the opportunity. The next time the offer presented itself, I would know that in order to avoid those negative feelings, I should pick up the phone and call. The images and words on screen are designed to *motivate* me to pick up my phone and dial the number on the screen.

As a leader, your job is to call people to action and then cause them to move. Once people move, they will stay in motion until something changes their course, slows them down or causes them to stop completely. When people are bored, tired or otherwise lethargic, they are difficult to set into motion in the first place and once they do move, there are always forces at the ready to slow them down. It is human nature to find a "safe" place and stay there. The problem is that when one stays there, nothing happens. Nothing gets done. A great leader stirs people's hearts, inspiring them to move toward something bigger than themselves. Leaders are not just in the business of moving people, they are in the business of getting people to move *themselves*. In regard to physics and inertia, most people do need that initial push out the door, so to speak. They need someone to believe in them and to tell them that they have the potential to create something positive and beneficial in their lives. Real leaders provide that first bit of momentum… that indefinable *something* that turns into perpetual motion in someone's life. Though a leader may not be present physically in a person's life, the initial inspiration a leader provides stays with a person either consciously or subconsciously throughout that person's life, and a leader's continued influence can create continual positive change when a "course correction" is needed. The inspired person then begins to affect those around them as the leadership energy transfers from that person to those in their sphere of influence. Eventually, key moments are created, movements are born, lives are changed. One leader can set this process in motion. Inertia.

One year after my failure in sixth grade reading, I met a man named Neil Jeffrey. Neil was the youth pastor at Prestonwood Baptist Church in Dallas TX, a church I began attending in seventh grade. Neil had been a star quarterback in college and in the NFL despite the fact that he had a speech impediment which caused him to stutter when he spoke. Calling plays, a key quarterback responsibility, was an almost unbearable task for him but he found a way to do it and to eventually become a dynamic and engaging speaker. Although there were hundreds of junior high and high school students in our youth group, Pastor Neil knew me by name and always made it a point to stop what he was doing and greet me whenever I came around. Over the next few years, I watched him… I paid attention to every word he said not just in his sermons, but in his conversations with other students and with me in particular. I was fascinated by the fact that a man who had once suffered from such a debilitating condition was now speaking to hundreds of people a week from the stage. I thought that perhaps if Neil could overcome this challenge in his life, I could overcome the barriers in my own. As I mentioned before, I was extremely shy, socially awkward, and not exactly the most popular kid in the group… but I knew that for some reason, I *mattered* to Neil Jeffrey. I wasn't just a name and a face, I was someone important enough to Neil that once, when a particularly difficult situation arose in my family, he left work to come visit me and shoot baskets with me in my back yard. He wanted to make sure I was okay. Over the course of the next few years, I began to change dramatically. I stopped being afraid of people, and I embraced my own personality to such a degree that I began to actually *enjoy* speaking in front of the youth group, leading discussions, and teaching younger students. Speaking in public began to feel like second nature to me… I began to love it. Although Neil and I had only a handful of "deep" conversations over the years, I can look back and say with complete sincerity that this man's influence on my life was the catalyst that caused me to go from being terrified of a room of sixth-graders, to being comfortable on a stage in front of thousands.

Leaders come and go in peoples' lives, but the leaders that *matter* are the ones who have such an impact on the lives of individuals that these people are literally changed forever. Despite the outside forces pressing against them, the person is propelled forward because of the influence of leaders in their life and the inspiration they continue to have along the way. This book is about becoming one of those leaders.

Inertia is…

Intent

Necessity

Energy

Resilience

Trust

Imagination

Authenticity

Chapter 1:

"Intent"

"Our intention creates our reality."

– Dr. Wayne Dyer

As I sit here typing at my computer, the intent of my mind is being transferred into practical, tangible motion: the movement of my fingers over the keyboard. Electrical signals in my brain are telling the muscles in my fingers to flex and contract, eventually producing digital words on a screen. I intend for movement to happen, and it happens. Simple cause-and-effect. An effective leader must have the *intent* to lead. Leadership is not an accident and it doesn't happen by chance. The legendary coach Vince Lombardi once said, "Leaders aren't born, they are made." A three-year-old with leadership potential is not a leader until she decides to step forward at some point in her life and actually lead others. When you ask a child what they want to be when they grow up, do they reply, "I want to be a great leader?" Not often. Typically they will say something like "fireman," "doctor," or even "president," all jobs which require a high level of leadership. The word "leader" is not a job in and of itself; it is more of a job *description*.

Some will argue that many great leaders never really wanted to become leaders, but were somehow "forced" into a leadership role. This idea of the "reluctant leader" is romantic, but not entirely realistic. When you look back at great historical leaders, you will see that even though some were not actively seeking a leadership role, once the opportunity was presented to them, they *intentionally* and *deliberately* began to lead. Of course, some of the best leaders have had to "warm up" to the idea of leading, but eventually they made conscious decision to do so. They have something bigger and greater in mind, but leadership becomes the *means* to their goals. The original intent is to accomplish an objective say, "making the world a better place." If making the world a better place were your goal, you would quickly discover that actually making this happen will require some help. It will take personnel, organization, planning and yes, leadership. At the point at which you decide that you will begin the task of changing the world for the better by inviting others to join you, and then motivating them to assist you in your calling, leadership itself becomes an integral part of the objective. You *intend* to lead.

Remember, effective leadership does not emerge from a desire to simply lead for its own sake, but out of a desire to accomplish a bigger goal or set of goals. This is a concept that is often difficult for "followers" to understand. It is often the perspective of those without leadership inclination to assume that if you desire to be a leader, then you must be doing so out of a desire for power. While this is sometimes the case, it is the exception rather than the rule. Author David Cooper says, "Perhaps the most central characteristic of authentic leadership is the relinquishing of the impulse to dominate others." A leader can absolutely intend to lead without any desire to dominate others or to make others subservient to their will. And as I mentioned before, some who become leaders don't initially intend to lead, but at some point they must make the conscious choice to do so. At the point at which you decide that you are ready to lead, it is a good time to ask yourself *why* you want to lead and what you desire to accomplish.

This past summer, I had some time on my hands, in fact, I had so much time that I created a giant ball completely out of rubber bands. Anyone who has ever created a nice big rubber band ball can tell you three things: 1. It is awesome. 2. It is a relaxing and Zen-like endeavor and 3. It takes a while. So with the time I had available, I created a ball weighing four pounds and spanning eight inches in diameter. People have often asked me how I started the ball and the answer is pretty simple: "I started with one rubber band!" I took that one rubber band, rolled it up into a tiny ball and began wrapping other rubber bands around it. As I type this sentence I am looking down on the floor at my beautiful multicolored rubber band ball (which you can see, by the way, on the front and back covers of this book.) As I mentioned, the ball is quite heavy and in general, quite stationary. However, every once in a while, my cat Keebler will walk by the ball, stare at it for a bit and then take a few good swipes, thereby jarring it from it's resting place and sending it rolling slowly across the wooden floor. Not only does this illustrate the idea of intent, but it reinforces the idea of inertia. Because of Keebler's intent (to move the ball,) his action (swiping) applied an outside force to the non-moving ball, causing it to become an object in motion. Now if Keebler weren't so easily bored, he might continue pawing at the ball, but usually he just walks away after a few good hits. Since there is no more of Keebler's intent/action causing the ball to keep rolling, the forces of gravity and friction take hold of it, causing it to stop rolling.

Notice that intent is not enough to cause action, but it is the *impetus* for the action. Plenty of people intend to do good things without ever actually doing them. Intent has to be combined with action, but without intent, there is no action. So how does this translate into leadership? I think a good place to start might be to ask yourself the question "Do I intend to lead?" Do you have the motivation to lead? If you believe that you have leadership potential but are not yet ready to assume an active leadership role, that's okay! It may not yet be your time. Utilize this period of your life to watch, listen, and learn from other leaders. The wisdom and experience you will gain while observing and preparing will be invaluable to you at the point at which you do accept your first true leadership role. However, if you do believe that your time for active leadership has come, then move forward boldly without glancing back. Your intent to lead must be present and powerful. Again, you will not become an effective leader by accident or by chance.

I am a huge fan of the Sci-Fi Channel's reworked version of the 70's TV show *Battlestar Galactica*. The new version is gritty, edgy, and well-made. Whereas the 70's show was campy and undeniably silly, the new version takes itself very seriously. One of the central characters on the show is Laura Roslin, played splendidly by actress Mary McDonnell. At the beginning of the series, Roslin is the secretary of education for the Twelve Colonies of Kobol, a confederation of civilized planets. The position is a comparatively low-level one with very limited power. When the colonies are attacked by the robotic race known as Cylons, Roslin becomes president by default when all eleven of her superiors are killed. The destruction of the colonies leaves only forty-thousand survivors, all of whom are aboard spaceships which quickly evacuate the solar system for the far reaches of space. Though Laura Roslin never intended to be president, she realizes quickly that she must now take on the role as the leader of all humanity. Over the course of the show's first season, she becomes a very powerful and effective president and much of the series' plotlines revolve around her. Now, one might say that Roslin became a leader accidentally and that she had no intent to become president. This is true, however, the writers of the show go out of their way in one of the early episodes to show that she was *already* a tough, tenacious, and effective leader even in the low position of secretary of education. As the secretary she defused a volatile teacher's strike and fell into disfavor with the previous president by doing so. She did not intend to become president herself, but she did intend to lead, and that intention is what eventually makes her into a great president and a great leader. In the case of Laura Roslin, her intent to lead, regardless of her title or position gave her the foundation for effective leadership. Eventually, however, that intent had to be realized in a tangible way; it had to become action.

My brother-in-law John Gelman is the head chef at a prominent historical resort hotel in downtown Austin, TX. Needless to say, he knows what he is doing in the kitchen. This past Christmas, I was visiting with my family in Austin and my sister Sibyl revealed that she had a very special present in store for me… several pounds of Giant Australian Prawns. Now, to call these things "shrimp" would be an understatement. In reality, they were each almost nine inches long! My sister knows that I am a shrimp fanatic, and so this was a wonderful gift. The next day, John marinated the shrimp and cooked them up on the grill. Even though I knew I was going to be working out and jogging within the hour, I decided to eat a bunch of the giant shrimp for lunch. Any reasonable person could tell you that loading up on several pounds of barbecued shrimp right before a four-mile run is not a wise decision, and my choice to do so proved to be a big mistake. About twenty minutes into my jog, I began to feel heavy and weak. Any runner knows the familiar feeling when your legs just don't want to move very quickly. At this point, I had to make a decision: I could either slow down, walk, stop, or keep running. It was the classic situation of "the spirit is willing but the flesh is weak." It is in moments like this where intent becomes the motivating force behind action. I decided that I would neither stop nor slow down. I decided that I would fight through the weakness and run faster. I consciously *willed* my legs to move more quickly and they did. I steadied my breathing, worked on my balance, smoothed out my steps, and quickened my pace despite the fact that my body wanted me to stop. When you decide that you truly want to lead, that you are motivated to do so, you must constantly and consciously *intend* to move forward. Deciding at some point that you want to be a leader is not enough. You must be in a continual state of intention toward becoming a better and stronger leader.

If you have the intent to lead, you have already taken the first and possibly the most important step toward actually making it happen. I assume that since you are reading this book and have made it this far, you do already have the intent firmly in place, so here are some practical steps to apply "intent" to your leadership:

1) **Define your intent.**

Ask yourself the basic "W" questions:

- **Whom** do I want to lead?

- **What** do I want to accomplish as a leader?

- **When** do I want to begin leading?

- **Where** do I want to lead?

- **Why** do I want to lead?

Write down your answers and refer back to them on a daily basis. See if they need to be modified or updated to match where you are on any given day. Writing down goals is one of the key elements to making them happen. When you are not looking your goals squarely in the eye, so to speak, it is easy to forget about them. It is nearly impossible to hit a target that you cannot see. Sometimes it helps to hear these goals as well, either from yourself or from someone whom you trust. I know it seems a little ridiculous to talk to oneself in the mirror, but I have done that very thing several times in recent memory with good results!

2) **Seek wise counsel.**

Look for someone whom you consider to be a skilled leader and ask them the same "W" questions about their leadership. People love to discuss their own successes, and you will find that true leaders are always willing to share their strategies and techniques. You may also discover some unique similarities that can help you see your own leadership strengths and weaknesses in a new light.

3) **Think big.**

Effective leaders don't simply intend to meet a *single* goal. They build upon their successes and defeats and are constantly in the process of setting newer, bigger goals for themselves. Intend to be the absolute best at whatever it is you want to do.

I was talking to a friend the other day about people who run for President of the United States. Though we disagreed on politics in general, we agreed that *everyone* who declares their intent to run for president *has* to possess some level of insanity in order to do so. If you think about what someone is saying when they declare themselves a candidate for president, they are essentially saying "I am uniquely qualified to be the most powerful and influential person in the world." That's a pretty intense declaration! If any "normal" person were to say something like this most people would call that person crazy, but when a presidential candidate says it, he is called visionary. Which is he? Perhaps both. The point is that our intent must be so powerful that it drives us to say and do things that others might view as less-than-logical. Your intent to lead may not seem feasible or prudent to those around you, but if that intent is there, feed it... nurture it... give it room to grow and flourish! You may be the quiet one in staff meetings who hardly ever speaks a word, and to some, the thought of you becoming a leader might seem like a fantasy. Again, however, keep in mind that once you do have the intent to lead, you have already taken a significant step forward. At the point at which you make this decision, you have already moved past the point where most people stop. The vast majority of individuals in the world are content to follow the leadership of others without giving a second thought to the idea that they themselves might actually have the ability, talent, or experience to lead. Sure they might *say* they could "do it better," but few really *believe* it and even fewer have the courage to step forward and actually *do* anything. I say let them stay where they are! I think it goes without saying that there are more than enough "armchair quarterbacks" in our world today who are content to sit back and throw stones while accomplishing nothing. Let them stay there. If you are a genuine leader, it is time for you to come forth and give physical, tangible form to that intent you hold within your heart.

Chapter 2:

"Necessity"

"Leadership involves finding a parade and getting in front of it."
– John Naisbitt

I am an unapologetic Dallas Cowboys fan and I have been my whole life. My mother dressed me in Cowboys blue and silver when I was three years old and I have the photos to prove it. I've been a fan through the good years (the 90s) and the bad years (most seasons since '96.) On October 23, 2006, an interesting thing happened in the Cowboys' world. Tony Romo, the Cowboys' second string quarterback got his big chance when coach Bill Parcels pulled starting quarterback Drew Bledsoe from the game at half-time and put Romo in the driver's seat against the New York Giants. On his first pass of the game, the ball was tipped and intercepted. Romo quickly regained his composure and ended up throwing fourteen completions for 227 yards and two touchdowns. Although his performance in that game was by no means perfect, it was impressive enough that two days later, Coach Parcels announced that Romo was going to be the Cowboys' starting quarterback for the foreseeable future. One year later on October 29, 2007, the Cowboys signed Romo to a six-year contract extension worth $67.5 million. Today Tony Romo is a household name and is considered one of the top quarterbacks in the league.

Obviously Romo had the intent to become a top-tier NFL quarterback. That's what all football players dream about as children. It is why they ask for footballs for Christmas and why they attend two-a-day practices in the heat of the summer in junior high. However, what Tony Romo was lacking up until the game against New York was the *necessity* for his leadership as a quarterback. It's not just about being in the "right place at the right time," which he was, it's about *recognizing* the necessity for your leadership, stepping boldly into the position, and then showing those around you that you truly belong there.

When a company or organization begins to fail, one of the first problems critics tend to point out is a "leadership vacuum," a lack of leadership. Things are not getting done, workers are not being inspired, the company is losing money. Regardless of whether or not this is the current leader's fault, the perception tends to be that it is. Either way, a leadership vacuum offers other people the opportunity to step in and take over. Now, here is the key to the idea of necessity: As a leader, you must put yourself into position so that when the opportunity does present itself, you are the one who can step in to fill the gap. Understand that I am not talking about doing anything dishonest or unethical. I am talking about doing positive things that over time will set you apart when *your* time comes. I truly believe that you can achieve a great deal of success without doing so at the expense of others. In fact, I decided long ago that if being successful meant stepping on others to get there, then I would rather be unsuccessful. I've found, however, that even though leaders do often have to make difficult decisions which affect some people in negative ways, exceptionally effective leaders achieve success not at the expense of others but because of their *benefit* to others.

Ask yourself honestly what benefit you are to those around you. Do you help the people in your charge or do you make their lives more difficult? Are you an asset to your company or are you a liability? If you were put into a higher position of authority within your organization, would it be a positive step for the organization or just for you? Leadership should always involve a symbiotic relationship. When a good leader is in place, everybody wins. Too many leaders seek positions of authority for the sake of the authority. The problem is, when they have only their own interests in mind, they will prosper at the *expense* of their company not to its benefit. The irony is, even though they may see a short-term benefit to their poor leadership motivation, when the organization begins to decline, they will suffer all the more and will eventually go down with the ship. On the other hand, when a leader sees the necessity for leadership, steps in with the good of the company in mind, fills the gap effectively, and shows those around him that it was a good choice to put him in the leadership position, the organization grows and prospers.

So in reality, this concept of necessity in regard to leadership is not just about taking advantage of an opportunity, it is a three-step process:

1) Prepare

Preparation takes time, sometimes lots of time. Noted author Malcolm Gladwell believes that to truly become a "master" at anything, it takes ten-thousand hours of practice. It won't matter if a window of opportunity opens for you if you are not prepared for it when it does. In Tony Romo's case, he had been playing football continuously for over *fifteen years* before the Cowboys handed him the reigns. That's a lot of time throwing balls, working out, and studying plays to prepare for that one big shot. Preparation takes a great deal of discipline. As you prepare for your leadership opportunities, you will probably do some extremely boring, menial, and seemingly unnecessary things in the meantime. I can think of a long list of ridiculous things I did as part of jobs I had before I ever had any kind of leadership responsibility, things such as:

- Slicing hundreds of purple onions at Burger Street restaurant in high school. (My finger-tips stayed purple and smelled like onions for at least twenty-four hours after slicing onions.)

- Babysitting on Friday nights for a steadily growing family who lived down the street from me. (I never got a pay increase, despite the fact that the family managed to produce a new child every nine months.)

- Mowing yards with four-foot high grass for $10 a yard.

- Refereeing flag football games for fraternities and sororities in college. (Sorority girls were the worst... there were moments of genuine hostility and threatened violence toward me because of some of my calls in those games.)

- Attempting to teach inner-city Chicago children how to sail at summer camp when most of them didn't even know how to swim.

While none of these activities, at the time, seemed to have *anything* to do with leadership, they all built my character in some way and in that regard, *directly* contributed to my leadership later in life. (Well... maybe not the onions.)

I love the phrase "Luck is when preparation and opportunity meet." (Roy D. Chapin, Jr.) If you turn the phrase into a simple mathematical formula you get: Preparation + Opportunity = Luck. Notice that of the two elements "Preparation" and "Opportunity," the former is the sole responsibility of the *individual*. In order to prepare, you must intend to prepare. The "opportunity" part may be partially or completely out of your hands, but the preparation is up to you. People often remark about successful people that they are "lucky" to be where they are. Well, if you view that through this formula, the "luck" they appear to have comes from not just a random set of circumstances, but in part, as a result of their preparation and intent.

2) Recognize

All the preparation in the world can't help you if you fail to see opportunities for leadership when they do present themselves. This might be the most difficult part of the formula. Some people spend so much time practicing and preparing that they simply do not recognize that there IS a need for them to step into the leadership role. The day-to-day activities of life have a way of lulling us into a comfortable routine. Going to work, taking the kids to soccer practice, watching our favorite TV shows... these are the kinds of things that can cause us to miss out on chances to lead if we are not paying close attention. Listen to what people around you are saying. Volunteer to help out, even if it's not in the top leadership role. As people begin to notice you and see your talents and skills, you will become an asset. If you are paying attention, you will see the necessity for leadership all around you and you will recognize that it is *you* who has the ability to fulfill that leadership role. Tony Romo had been practicing with the Cowboys for more than two full seasons but had never thrown a pass in a regular-season game until the game against New York. He had put in the practice time but he was also watching closely for the right moment to step in.

3) Move

This is the part that really takes guts. Again, you can prepare and you can recognize an opportunity, but if you do not physically take that leap of faith and step into the role, you will miss it. It's like having a beautiful, fine-tuned racecar out on the track ready for the race, and then failing to hit the gas pedal when the flag drops. This ties back into the idea of intent. In fact, intent *becomes* action. You must decide ahead of time what you will do when the door opens. You must know beyond all doubt that if you are given the chance, you will take it. Even the best of us often fail "in the moment" because we have not decided ahead of time what specific action we will take.

Over the years I have seen an interesting strategy put forth by decidedly weak, unqualified leaders, that of manufacturing a necessity for their leadership. Plato once said, "A tyrant is always stirring up some war or other, in order that the people may require a leader." Though this tactic may work in the short-term, I believe that this is actually counter-productive to effective leadership. Leaders who manipulate circumstances so that their "leadership" becomes necessary do so for their own benefit and not for the benefit of those whom they serve. I do believe in cause-and-effect, sowing-and-reaping, or what some would call "karma." When your motives are selfish, your product will be morally weak. As I have explained in this chapter, true leaders work on building experience and character within themselves, so that they will be prepared when their time comes. When you try to "cheat the system" you ultimately end up with failure. Weakness is always exposed, and usually exploited, in the end.

Once you have prepared and once you see a leadership gap, step boldly into the breach. Let the "powers that be" know that you will lead without reservation. Take whatever tools that are given to you, even if they be weak or few, and combine them with the experience you have gained over time and make it happen! Do not hesitate, do not pause, do not fear. Be bold, be strong, be courageous!

Chapter 3:

"Energy"

"Big thinkers are specialists in creating positive, forward-looking, optimistic pictures in their own minds and in the minds of others."

- David J. Schwartz

I have a niece named Katherine, and she is one of my favorite people in the entire world. She recently turned five and many people wonder if she is ever going to slow down. You see, Katherine has exactly two modes: "Full Speed Ahead" or "Asleep." There really is no middle ground with this kid. She was practically born running and by all estimates, she won't be easing up any time soon. I don't yet have any children of my own, but I am not sure that I could handle one if he or she had half the energy of my niece. I'm only thirty-five but one afternoon with Katherine at the park or the mall or Chuck E. Cheese makes me feel like I should be receiving my AARP card at any moment. For her, the energy is part physical and part emotional. At five years old she SHOULD have a surplus of energy, but in addition to the physical energy, she has an intangible emotional electricity and passion for life that is absolutely contagious. I find that although she makes me physically exhausted, I love being around her because she elevates my mood and makes me want to be a better uncle.

Now, when I talk about energy in terms of leadership, I'm not merely referring to physical energy or stamina, although that type of energy is important because who likes a tired leader, right? I'm talking more about the positive or negative "vibe" that you portray to others. When you walk into a room, how do people respond to you? Do they avoid you or do they tend to gravitate toward you? As I mentioned, my niece Katherine embodies both types of energy. She has boundless physical, kinetic energy, but more importantly, she brightens any room with her sheer presence. As a leader, it is essential to create and maintain an air of positive energy.

When I was a youth minister, and the church was my life, Sunday mornings were always a bittersweet time for me. On one hand, I looked forward to seeing my students and leading them through whatever activities were planned for that particular day, but on the other hand, I knew that every Sunday morning brought people into my path whom I tried desperately to avoid. I'm sure you have these types of people in your life as well; the kind of people you really do go out of your way to avoid because they suck the life out of you. Now to be fair, these people were certainly in the minority, but such a *vocal* minority. Do you know the kind of people I'm talking about here? People who constantly complain, whine, and argue about everything for no good reason? These people are clearly miserable but they won't settle for that, they want to make everyone around them miserable as well. These people often fancy themselves to be "helpful" or "informative" individuals, and they usually don't even recognize the negativity that pervades their lives. These people are the main reason that good leaders leave. It's not surprising to me at all that the average tenure of a Christian minister at one particular church is eleven months! Churches are a lot like hospitals… lots of patients, comparatively few doctors.

Although Sunday mornings often brought me into contact with individuals who did everything within their power to bring me down emotionally, spiritually, even physically, to their level, there were also people like my friend Mike Cortines who did exactly the opposite. In the eight years that I spent in ministry at Harbor Point Community Church, I can say that the most influential person in my life was Pastor Mike. Now Mike and I didn't spend a lot of time sitting around having "heavy" conversations. Most of our interactions were pretty casual and light, but it wasn't Mike's words that influenced me as much as it was his persona, his energy. While I was at Harbor Point, I never once saw Mike get angry. I never saw him lose his cool, and I never heard him say a hurtful thing about anyone. He didn't gossip, he didn't try to advance his career at the expense of others, he just *loved* people, especially children, and went out of his way to make the lives of others a little better every day. Just being in his presence was uplifting to me. His smiles, his jokes, his punches in the arm, his daily greeting of "Hey B-Man!"... these were the things that made Mike a great leader in the church. He didn't give eloquent sermons or long, pious prayers, he just cared. The positive energy he displayed on a daily basis was an amazing motivator for me. In Dr. Wayne Dyer's book, *The Power of Intention*, he says, "Choose to be in close proximity to people who are empowering, who appeal to your sense of connection to intention, who see the greatness in you, who feel connected to God, who live a life that gives evidence that Spirit has found celebration through them." It is my great hope to have the influence on others that Mike Cortines had on me.

Let's do a quick experiment here. I want you to think of one person about whom you can say the following things:

1) This person is someone whom I consider to be an exceptional leader.

2) This person has had a profound impact on my life.

3) I have physically met this person.

In thinking about this person, ask yourself how you felt the last (or only) time you were with him. Did you feel inspired, enthusiastic, or energetic in her presence? When you were around this person, what kind of energy would you say he exuded? I would venture to say that when you were near this person you felt a positive attraction to, as well as a positive vibe in his or her presence. For the vast majority of you reading this, I believe you would say that this person makes you feel, well, good! Of course you would. Although I'm sure there are a few notable exceptions, leaders are *positive* people.

From where does this positive energy come? Is it just part of one's personality or is it something that develops over time? Though some people have a natural inclination toward the positive or negative, I believe their energy is greatly determined by habit and repetition. Their outward energy comes from their internal energy. How we view the world determines how we affect the world! If we see life from a primarily negative point of view, it is virtually impossible to have a positive affect on circumstances or people around us. Again, it's back to a simple formula: Garbage in = Garbage out. Yes, I know it's an old cliché but clichés persist because of the kernels of truth they often contain. If my thoughts are negative, my actions will be negative as well and I will not be an effective leader. Another interesting idea about the concept of positive energy is how little it takes to create positive change.

Think of the last time someone gave you a compliment. What was it this person complimented you on? Your looks? Your clothes? Something you had accomplished at work? (If you can't think of the last time someone complimented you, then you definitely need to find some positive people to spend some time with!) On the other hand, think of how devastating one rude comment can be. When someone insults your work, your intelligence or your appearance, that one off-handed remark can ruin your whole day and possibly have long-lasting negative effects. How much do negative people really accomplish? Although they have the ability to bring others down fairly quickly, over time their negativity loses its effect because people eventually begin to ignore it! I find it very easy to ignore negative people but almost impossible to ignore positive people! Great leaders radiate positive energy. That's their job! How are leaders of nations, corporations, or organizations so effective? Because they infuse positive, constructive energy into everyone around them.

The image of the "motivational speaker" has become a cliché over the years (thanks in part to comedian Chris Farley's brilliant skits as "Matt Foley" on *Saturday Night Live* who "lived in a VAN down by the RIVER!"), but the reality is that motivational speakers *motivate people*! The message of the motivational speaker is almost always about positive thinking and positive perception producing positive action. Real leaders understand that hope is a stronger motivator than fear. Many would not consider the French General Napoleon Bonaparte to have been a "positive" leader, but he knew how to motivate people. He knew the power of positive energy and motivation when he said, "A leader is a dealer in hope." When I think of great leaders, I don't think of "gloom and doom" nay-sayers, I think of "I have a dream," "Ask not what your country can do for you," and "All we need is love."

Consider this the next time you are at the office water cooler and you are tempted to unleash a well-earned tirade against your boss. Were you to say what's on your mind, how will you come across to those around you? What type of energy would you be radiating at that point through your words and actions? I understand that none of us can be positive *all* the time. That's not what I'm talking about. I'm talking about your demeanor, your posture, your tone of voice– all the factors that combine to form that intangible energetic force. That force affects those in your vicinity whether you want it to or not. Both positivity and negativity are extremely contagious, so not only will people around you notice your energy, they will absorb it and begin to emit it themselves. Rachel Maddow, one of my favorite personalities on CNN sums up the concept of positive attraction in leadership quite nicely: "Humans are ambitious and rational and proud. And we don't fall in line with people who don't respect us and who we don't believe have our best interests at heart. We are willing to follow leaders, but only to the extent that we believe they call on our best, not our worst."

One of the most fascinating things about energy is that according to the laws of physics, energy cannot be destroyed, only transferred. (I love thinking about this in terms of music and sound. By this line of thinking, every note that has ever been played in the history of the world is still floating around somewhere in the universe in one form of energy or another.) So think about this: all the energy you transfer to another person whether positive or negative, stays with that person forever.

A few years ago I got a job working as a tour manager for a large American vacation company. The company specialized in overseas tours, and I was trained to run tours in southern Italy. Initially this seemed like the ultimate dream job. I would be working in one of the most beautiful and historically significant regions of the world, traveling full-time, meeting new people on a daily basis, and enriching the lives of others by promoting cultural awareness and understanding. Now, all of these things proved to be true, but they were, in many ways, negated by the people I ended up having to deal with. This particular company catered to the "retiree" crowd. Most of the people who went on my tours were age sixty or over. Keep in mind that prior to this job, I had spent most of my professional career working with students. Let's just say there was a bit of a "generational gap" between me and my clients.

The basic gist of this job was that I would meet groups of forty or so American tourists in Italy (usually in Rome), put them on a coach (tour bus), and escort them around the country for two weeks. I was responsible for getting them to dozens of destinations along the way including hotels, restaurants, and tourist attractions. I was required to have an in-depth knowledge of the country, the people, the language, the food, and pretty much anything and everything in Italy. Although my official job title was "Tour Manager," I functioned as a valet, a paramedic, a counselor, a logistician, an entertainer, a professor, and performed many other unique and often unrelated duties. For instance, one night when my passengers (twenty retired New York City firemen and their wives) arrived in Catania, Sicily, I was quickly informed that ALL of their luggage had been left behind in Rome because of a labor strike. It became my responsibility to not only locate and retrieve more than forty suitcases, but to care for the needs of my passengers who had been traveling for twenty-four hours in some cases, and who had nothing with them but the clothes on their backs. The rest of that night involved me running around a small village in Sicily buying every toothbrush and tube of toothpaste I could find while somehow managing to get all of my passengers checked into the hotel and seated at their evening meal. I stayed up all night dealing with the situation and then, once the luggage did finally arrive the next morning, I packed all forty passengers into our coach to begin the tour. Despite the madness of that night, what I remember most about the ordeal was how ungrateful the passengers were. I had managed to pull off a feat of epic proportions and yet I don't remember anyone offering me so much as a simple "thank you." Some of them probably did thank me, but I don't remember that. What I DO remember is the whining, moaning, complaining, and yelling that the passengers did when they were inconvenienced by not having their bags ready for them that night. Obviously, I had nothing to do with the labor strike or their lost bags, but I bore the brunt of their anger and frustration.

What had once seemed like a dream job quickly turned into a nightmare. I did ten such tours over the course of a year and in every single group, there were a handful of people who, it seemed, had been sent there by God (or Satan) to test every fiber of my patience, character, and decency. Over the course of the year, their negative energy simply wore me down, and I had to walk away from the job. I regret the fact that I let negative people have such a profound influence on me, but in actuality, the experience has made me appreciate even more the amazing power of positive leadership. As a leader, it is your job to create an environment of positivity so that those around you are lifted up.

The force that a leader applies to someone's life is not a force of coercion, it is a force of *inspiration*. Unfortunately, people, in general, face a lot more negativity in their lives than positivity. When negative forces act against people, they can cause people to fall, to give up, or to settle for less than they should in life. The exceptional leader inspires people to such a degree that even though negative forces rise up against them, the passion, drive, ideas, and energy they received from the leader help them to press through the negative. Energy and enthusiasm go hand in hand, and in order to be an effective leader, you *must* be enthusiastic not just about an idea, but about *your* ability to turn that idea into reality. One of the greatest qualities of enthusiasm is that it has the power to destroy apathy! Arnold Toynbee explained that although enthusiasm can destroy apathy, enthusiasm itself is generated by "an ideal, which takes the imagination by storm," and by "a definite intelligible plan for carrying that ideal into practice." Ralph Waldo Emerson said, "Nothing great was ever achieved without enthusiasm." I would challenge you to think of someone who disproves that concept! If you *can* think of someone, I will show you fifty *more* people who pursued something with all their hearts and inspired those around them to join them to a great and glorious end! You must have passion, you must have enthusiasm, you must have energy. Sometimes, however, these plans fail initially and must be developed carefully over time. That brings us to…

Chapter 4:

"Resilience"

"Don't call it a comeback... I've been here for years."

- LL Cool J

Frank Sinatra was the greatest American entertainer of all time. Anyone who knows me knows that not only do I believe this, but I will happily and enthusiastically debate anyone who begs to differ with me. Sinatra was a superstar before there really was such a thing in popular culture. A consummate entertainer, "Ol' Blue Eyes" created hundreds of hit records from 1943's "All or Nothing at All" to his most famous tune, 1969's "My Way." He sold millions upon millions of albums, won thirteen Grammy's, starred in fifty-eight feature films, as well as dozens of popular television specials. Sinatra was popular with everyone– young, old, men, women (including "A-List" lovers Ava Gardner, Mia Farrow, and Lauren Bacall.) No one before or since has or will ever come close to achieving the amount of success and influence in the entertainment world as Sinatra achieved. All that being said, he was also one of the most resilient characters in the history of entertainment.

When you look at the timeline of Frank's life, you can see that he actually had *three* separate successful careers. He became a star in the early forties, especially with the "bobby soxers" (girls), and climbed swiftly to the top of the charts where he reigned for a good portion of the 1940's. By the early fifties, his popularity had waned to such an extent that in 1952 both his record label (Columbia) and his booking agency (MCA) completely dropped him from their rosters. At this point, lesser men would have counted their cash and left the game, but not Frank. Instead, he sought out a new recording label and returned again to the silver screen alongside Burt Lancaster in 1953's *From Here to Eternity*, for which Sinatra won the Best Supporting Actor Oscar for his moving portrayal of Private Angelo Maggio. In 1953, he signed with Capitol Records, re-invented himself and returned, once-again, to the top of the charts with albums such as *In the Wee Small Hours*, and *Frank Sinatra Sings For Only The Lonely*, which earned him the number one spot again and remained on the *Billboard* chart for 120 consecutive weeks. After thirty-six years in the music business, Sinatra retired in 1971... for two years. In 1973 he returned to the stage and screen where he rose to the top of the charts yet again with eight more albums and continued to perform to packed houses until his death in 1998.

A successful leader has to know how to make a comeback. If you as a leader have not yet tasted the bitterness of a crushing, debilitating defeat, prepare yourself because it *will* happen. It is the nature of leadership and it is in the nature of those being led to build up and tear down their leaders. Expect it, and learn how to bounce back from it.

When you are defeated, you always have a choice. You can accept defeat and allow it to end your career, your relationships, even your life, OR you can use it as a stepping stone to your next level of success. The problem is that leaders, by nature, are often simply too sensitive and too impatient. We take defeat *extremely* personally and often see it as a sign that we should give up, that perhaps we never even deserved the success that we had achieved in the first place. In some ways, failure, and the accompanying emotions are *addictive*. When we hit a "streak" of difficult losses, we get used to it. We adapt by accepting failure as the norm, rather than the exception. It becomes easier to remain on the ground than to rise up again.

The beautiful thing about failure though, is that it can be the impetus for even greater success. Remember my giant rubber band ball I discussed in chapter one? Besides its inherent coolness, the ball has an unusual amount of bounciness! Like I mentioned, the ball is quite heavy and one would expect it to have very little resilience because of its size and weight. However, with a little bit of force off of a hard, flat surface, the ball will easily bounce close to thirty feet into the air! Getting back to physics, the amount of compressed energy contained within the ball is multiplied many times over at the point of impact and this energy is quickly released, causing the ball to travel upward, swiftly moving past the place from which it was thrown and surpassing the distance several times over. Think about this in terms of leadership. When we fall, the amount of force applied to our fall can be translated directly into the height of our future success. This is such a liberating idea! When you know that every word spoken against you, every injustice you suffer, every dollar you lose, and every friend who betrays your trust contributes initially to that downward motion, but then, ultimately to your success, you will learn not to make such a big deal of those challenges in the first place. Not only will the ball bounce back, but it has *no choice* in the matter! It is a physical law that the ball will bounce back. The energy and material contained within the ball, combined with the downward force applied to it, make it physically impossible for the ball to not rocket toward the sky.

I was watching one of my favorite movies last night: *Rocky IV*. If you are male and grew up in the 80s, chances are you know this movie well. The film's plot is pretty standard: Hero's friend fights, hero's friend dies, hero avenges friend. Despite being a really solid action/sports movie in general, the film actually has some surprisingly poignant moments. One that comes to mind is an intense discussion between Rocky, standing at the bottom of a dimly-lit staircase, and his wife Adrian, standing at the top. Rocky is making the case to his wife as to why he *must* fight the Russian giant Ivan Drago, who has just killed his best friend Apollo Creed in the ring. Adrian knows that Rocky wants to avenge Apollo's death but she also knows that Rocky hasn't fought in a while. The dialog is telling:

Adrian: Why can't you change your thinking?

Everybody else does!

Rocky: Because I'm a fighter!

That's the way I'm made.

That's what you married.

Think carefully about what Rocky is saying. He cannot help but get in the ring because that is what he *does*. It is in his *nature* to fight and to bounce back. To do anything less would diminish who he is as a person. The debate continues:

Adrian: You've seen him. You know how strong he is.

You *can't win!*

Rocky: Maybe I can't win. Maybe the only thing I can do...

is just take everything he's got.

But to beat me, he'll have to kill me.

And to kill me...

he'll have to have the heart to stand in front of me.

And to do that...

he has to be willing to die himself.

I don't know if he's ready to do that.

Rocky acknowledges that he probably won't win the fight. He knows Drago's power and he has witnessed his ferocity up-close. Regardless, he will stand up to him and he will fight and he will take everything the Russian has... to whatever end. Rocky believes not in his ability to *win* the fight, but in his ability to stand and fight until the end.

As a leader, you will face more adversity than most. You will be a target. You will be hated by some for no reason other than because you are in the public eye. Many will transfer their own weaknesses and shortcomings to you and in some cases, you will fall. That much is certain. The question is, do you have the character, the resolve, and the inner strength to get up again and rise to a place that is higher than the place from which you fell?

Here are some interesting facts about some leaders you know:

- Abraham Lincoln was defeated in 1832 when he ran for the Illinois State Legislature, and again in 1858 for the US Senate before becoming President of the United States.

- Donald Trump has declared bankruptcy not once, but *three* times.

- Cyclist Lance Armstrong underwent cancer surgery and extensive chemo-therapy before winning the *Tour De France*... seven times in a row.

- Quarterback Brett Favre holds the records for most career touchdown passes, most career passing yards, most career pass completions, most career pass attempts, and...most career interceptions.

- Michael Jordan failed to make his high school varsity basketball team because at 5'11" he was "too short."

There are a hundred clichés I could throw out about rising from the depths of defeat, dusting yourself off and succeeding, but instead of doing that, let me tell you three things I myself try to do when I fail in my own life:

1) Be realistic.

I HATE losing. That doesn't make me unique, it makes me normal. However, nearly all defeats are temporary and of *much* less consequence than we think they are at the time. When you place a large amount of emotional stock in something you are doing and it ends up not working out the way you hoped it would, it often *feels* like the end of the world doesn't it? When we begin to see our failures for what they *really* are though, opportunities for learning and progress, then they can actually begin to make us better. Winston Churchill said, "Success consists of going from failure to failure without loss of enthusiasm." Do not lose hope. Be the rubber band ball! Sometimes, in order to get a clear perspective on things, however, it helps to…

2) Get a second opinion.

A leader needs to be able to hear other voices besides her own. Although you should rely primarily on your own thoughts and instincts, you should also establish a few select relationships with people who will tell you the truth, even if it hurts. Be careful though. Close friends and family members, although they do have our best interests at heart, are often too invested in our lives to be objective. Also, they tend to "soften" the hard facts so that they don't sting as much. They do this to protect us in the short term, but this is not always a good thing. As a leader, you need to be aware of your weaknesses, your short-comings, and yes, your failures. Otherwise, you will never improve. The brutal truth from a honest friend can be invaluable in becoming a stronger and more successful leader.

3) Take responsibility.

Even if the cause of your failure is largely due to someone else, determine which part of it was yours and OWN IT. The beauty of responsibility is that it gives the power back to you. If the problem is always someone else, then you are powerless to change anything! However, if there is something you can do to fix a situation in the future or to change your thoughts, motives, or behavior, then YOU are in control.

In order for an object to be resilient, it has to also have a certain amount of flexibility. Think of a plastic ruler. When you bend a ruler and release it, it immediately snaps straight but it is its inherent flexibility that allows it to bend in the first place. Regarding resilience as a leader, it is not just about bouncing back from defeat, it is also about being flexible in your leadership style to begin with. The French novelist Albert Camus once wrote, "Blessed are the hearts that can bend; they shall never be broken." No one wants to follow a leader who insists that his way is the only way and that all his policies are non-negotiable. Of course, there always eventually comes a time when a good leader *does* have to stand her ground, but in most situations, a bit of flexibility is a good thing. Flexibility shows those around you that their ideas matter too. People love to be a part of something big, they want to *belong* and an effective leader knows how to make people feel like they are a part of something big and that they do belong. When it comes down to it, leadership is about people. People are all different and they have unique ideas. One of the traits of effective leaders is the ability to gauge the will of the people, discover where they as leaders have similarities and differences, and to find a way to bring them together. The most famous leaders in history were the ones who brought people together, not the ones who scattered and fractured them. A strong but flexible leader knows how to be diplomatic, how to negotiate, and by doing so, how to build bridges and unite people for a common cause. As I said earlier, this flexibility will also serve you well when you fall, as it will contribute to your "bounce" back to success.

Chapter 5:

"Trust"

"No soul is desolate as long as there is a human being for whom it can feel trust and reverence."

- T.S. Eliot

If you could go back in a time machine and change one moment in your life, would you do it, and, if so, which moment would you change? I have asked many people this question and I have found that about half of the people I have asked would want to go back and half say they would not want to change anything. I certainly fall into the category of those who would absolutely choose to go back and change a moment or two. Actually, I have *several* events in my past that I would go back and change in a heartbeat if I could. Here is the one that makes the top of the list.

When I was eighteen, my Sunday school teacher David Holloman took me and my friends Steve and Jay on a camping trip to Arkansas to celebrate our upcoming graduation. Although we were all technically "adults," my friends and I still held on to some of the ridiculousness that comes with being a teenager and not really wanting to grow up. We were reckless and didn't pay a whole lot of attention to rules, safety precautions, or simple common sense.

On the second day of our trip, we set off into the woods with Mr. Holloman to hike up a mountain or two. (These were the Ozark mountains, not the Rockies, but they were somewhat challenging to hike.) As the day wore on, we veered from the path and began climbing on large rock formations on the side of the mountain. Throughout the day while we were hiking, we had seen large, thick vines hanging from the trees and wondered aloud whether or not these vines could hold us if we swung on them. I decided that I would answer this question for myself so I climbed up onto a ten-foot boulder, sliced the bottom of one of the vines and pulled on it to see if it would hold. It did. From there I grabbed a little higher on the vine and swung down from the rock to the ground without much effort. In our minds, we had answered the question. The vines could DEFINITELY hold us!

Not content with swinging from the rock, we decided to raise the stakes a bit. We hiked a little way up the mountain and found a ravine which descended about thirty feet down into a dried-up, rocky creek bed. Around the edges of the ravine, there were dozens of trees with hundreds of vines hanging from them. We had seen way too many movies to miss out on an opportunity to swing across a precipitous ravine on vines so that is exactly what we did. When one of us grabbed the vine and swung out over the ravine, we were at one point, thirty or more feet in the air, suspended above a creek bed consisting of flat granite rocks. This didn't trouble us very much because we trusted the vines. They hadn't failed us yet so why *shouldn't* we trust them?

We entertained ourselves swinging across the ravine for about thirty minutes and then decided that we should begin heading back to the campsite. It was at this exact point that I made a decision that if I could go back in a time machine and un-make, I would.

The guys started walking up the trail, and I yelled out, "One more time!" I then walked to the edge of the ravine, grabbed the vine, stepped back a few paces and then jumped, holding onto the vine. Now, as I said, we had been swinging on this vine for a good thirty minutes and the fact that we might have weakened it never crossed my mind until I was actually in mid-air, watching the vine unravel from the trees above. With nowhere to go but down, I fell thirty feet, landing on my feet on solid rock. In doing so I shattered my heel bone into a dozen or so pieces and broke two vertebrae in my back due to the massive compression caused by the impact.

I don't remember much of the rescue effort or the next few days for that matter because I was unconscious during most of the process. From what I have been told (many times) by my friends, they carried me about a mile to a trail and called the paramedics who carried me the rest of the way off the mountain and eventually drove me to a hospital.

I spent the next year on crutches as a number of doctors attempted to repair my foot through surgical means. One was eventually successful and I now walk with a very slight limp and don't feel any real discomfort in my foot. However, the injuries my back sustained in the accident have never healed completely. I still suffer from chronic back pain and probably always will.

The key element to this story is *trust*. Clearly, when I grabbed onto the vine and swung out over the ravine, I was putting my trust in the *wrong place*. Though the vine had sustained our antics for about thirty minutes, the vine was never *meant* to hold the weight of three teenagers and thus gave way eventually under the stress.

Ask yourself this question: As a leader, am I a "vine" that people can trust? Will I hold under the stress of leadership or will I snap when times get tough? An effective leader must be someone people can trust.

Where there is no trust, there is no leadership. The effectiveness of your leadership will grow in direct proportion to the amount of trust you are able to instill in those around you.

Trust is the absolute foundation of leadership. People will not follow someone whom they do not trust. Now they may *obey* an untrustworthy person, but they will not willingly submit to their leadership or consult them in times of need if they do not trust them wholeheartedly. Think about your car for a moment. What if you received an email report from your car's manufacturer today saying that your car has some serious technical flaws and that there is a 1-in-100 chance that the wheels will fall off when you drive it. Now statistically, the wheels probably won't fall off of your car. The odds are in your favor, but who in their right mind would accept them and continue driving the car without having the problem fixed? When you get into your vehicle, you *trust* that it is functional and safe. It is something you don't really think much about right? In actuality you are putting an amazing amount of trust in the machine. You trust it to start when you turn the key. You trust the engine to work. You trust the brakes to function when you press the pedal. You trust that the seatbelts and airbags will work correctly should you need them. What if you got in your car and discovered that the brakes only worked about half the time? Would you consider that to be acceptable or would you call a tow truck to take your car to the nearest repair facility immediately? Our trust for our leaders is very similar. We believe that they will lead us in the right direction. We believe they will work on our behalf. We believe *in them*.

In the mid-eighties, the religious community in the United States underwent a crisis of broken trust. Over the course of a few years, numerous big-name television evangelists like Jimmy Swaggart, Jim Baker, and Robert Tilton found themselves embroiled in a variety of scandals involving varying degrees of sexual and fiscal misconduct. These men had built multi-million dollar operations on the basis of their credibility and trustworthiness as leaders. People had looked to them for comfort and guidance and in the end, they betrayed the trust of these people and saw their own personal empires crumble around them as a result. Even though the evangelists involved in the scandals admitted their wrongdoing, the damage was done and they never came close to fully recovering.

Since that time, the American public has grown accustomed to unsavory behavior by religious, political, and corporate leaders, but at what cost? People simply do not trust leaders like they used to. The unfortunate fact is that because of a small percentage of disingenuous leaders, the trustworthy leaders have had to bear the brunt of the distrust and skepticism created by their predecessors. Trust is absolutely essential to leadership and because that trust has been corroded, we as leaders must work *extra* hard to not only build trust in our people, but to *maintain* that trust by our words and actions. When a leader betrays the trust of his people, his people interpret that as him putting his own personal needs ahead of theirs. When people believe that a leader would "sell them out" then they cease to trust that person. People need to know that their leader has their best interests at heart.

Lately I've been thinking about the phrase "trust is a crystal vase." The more I think about it, the more I realize that it is a stunningly accurate image used to describe the concept of trust. Consider the following comparison: Like a perfect crystal vase, trust is precious, valuable, and difficult to create. A good piece of crystal is a work of art. At holidays, weddings, or other special events, the hosts often bring out the crystal glasses, goblets, and dinnerware. They are special. Likewise, when you earn the trust of someone, you have earned something that money cannot buy. People need to trust their leaders. There are only a small handful of leaders in my life whom I trust explicitly, in fact, I can count them on one hand. These are people whom I know I could call at any time for any reason and they would not only give me good advice, but would go out of their way to help me. Do your employees, parishioners, students, or constituents have this level of trust in you? I know there are some people who do have this level of trust in me and I hope that I can continue to prove myself worthy of the trust they have placed in me. I know that over the years through some bad choices and through some unintended circumstances, some have lost their trust in me. Unfortunately, I will probably never regain the trust I lost.

Like a crystal vase, trust is easily broken. When a crystal vase breaks, it REALLY breaks! Typically, if a vase falls from a shelf or table, it shatters into thousands of tiny pieces. Crystal is fragile and it is in its nature to not just crack, but to shatter when it hits something solid. Trust is the same way. Usually it only takes one lie, one mistake, or one betrayal of confidence to completely destroy any amount of trust that may have taken a long time to establish.

I recently loaned a business associate a sizeable amount of money for a particular project. We had worked together on a daily basis for five months and I had come to trust him. I loaned him the money in good faith with the understanding and expectation that he would repay the loan within a certain period of time. He had expressed his intention to do so on numerous occasions but when he left the project we were working on, he stopped taking my calls and stopped answering my messages. A few days ago I found out through a third party that he has no intention of repaying the debt. Regardless of whether he does or doesn't, he has permanently lost my trust. Even if he were to show up at my door today with a check in hand, his actions destroyed the trust I had placed in him.

Finally, like a shattered vase, broken trust is nearly impossible to repair. When a piece of crystal is chipped or broken into a few large pieces, it can be repaired, usually at great cost. Restoration experts do have the ability to polish scratches, file down chips, or bond pieces of crystal back together but as I mentioned earlier, when a crystal vase falls, it doesn't break neatly in two, it explodes quite dramatically. When this happens, there is nothing anyone can do to repair the damage. The destruction is permanent and irreversible.

As I mentioned before, when the televangelists of the 80s fell, they fell hard and never recovered. They lost the trust of the people and their reputations were forever tarnished regardless of their apologies and pleas for forgiveness. People can forgive, but they rarely forget.

So far, the type of trust I've been speaking of has been of the moral variety. It may not be fair in all cases, but people do expect leaders to be "above the fray" in terms of morality. However, in the business world, trust is not simply a morality issue, but a competence issue as well. When a football team fails to make the playoffs, when a film bombs at the box-office, when a company's stock price falls, people lose trust. The fault may not lie with the coach, director, or CEO, but the public holds them responsible regardless because they are in charge. This is one of the burdens of leadership. As a leader, you will be accountable for failures that are not your fault. Sometimes, we cannot avoid loss of trust because things happen that are out of our control. What we can do, however, is to go out of our way to maintain our own personal and professional integrity in everything we do. This minimizes issues which can damage our reputation and the trust we have developed. Here are three key elements to establishing and maintaining the trust of those whom you serve through your leadership:

1) Choose your associates wisely.

It may not be fair but it is true that people will judge you by the company you keep. In leadership this is extremely important as it relates to trust. If you work for an organization and are constantly being seen in the company of someone who is known to be dishonest, disloyal, or even incompetent, people will eventually begin to associate those words with *you* through no real fault of your own. But aside from how outsiders perceive you and your associates, it is to your direct benefit to align yourself with people whom you can trust. Every leader needs someone to watch his back. One of your greatest assets as a leader is the group of people who will speak well of you behind your back! It is very easy to find people who will put you down when you are not around so that they themselves will be elevated, but a true ally is a rare find. Common wisdom dictates that you should keep your friends close and your enemies closer but I disagree. The people closest to you are the ones who will not only influence you the most (for better or for worse) but they will also be the ones to stand up for you when you are not present. If you want to be trusted as a leader, surround yourself with trustworthy people.

When I was in ministry, I had to learn this concept the hard way. Within the first year I learned that what people say about you truly matters. In some cases, it may matter even more than what you do or say yourself! As soon as I joined the staff at Harbor Point, I gathered together a small group of adult volunteers to help me build a youth group from the ground up. At the time, I thought that if someone volunteered to help work with kids, well that person's heart *had* to be in the right place. I was sorely mistaken. It soon became apparent that some of the people who had volunteered to "help out" only did so to watch me and report to others what I was doing as youth director. Their agenda was to come across as helpful when I was around, but to tear me down when I was not there. Over the years I realized that there were some people out there who didn't have the courage to share their "concerns" with me, but they sure didn't mind sharing them with others. Once I figured out what was going on, I began a systematic process of "weeding out" the destructive elements and bringing in volunteers who were loyal to me and to what I was doing.

2) Establish accountability in your own life.

Often, leaders will sequester themselves from the rest of their organization in an attempt to maintain some kind of privacy in their lives. On the surface, this makes sense but the problem is that the greater public will interpret this as you having "something to hide."

While there are some things that you obviously do need to keep private such as family matters, when it comes to your business, I am of the opinion that transparency is the best policy. If everything is out on the table, then you minimize people's curiosity and their tendency to convince themselves that their imaginations are factual. Often, leaders are way too touchy about "their business." They want to keep their lives completely private and while this *sounds* good, it is just not practical. When you become a leader, or any type of public figure for that matter, you must be willing to give up some of your privacy and anonymity.

At Harbor Point, I made a habit of keeping the door to my office open as much as possible. If I were counseling anyone, I would at least leave the door cracked. If I were having a conversation with a woman or young lady in my office, I always kept the door WIDE open not for my own benefit, but for the benefit of others. In the eight years I served as youth director, I was never once alone with a female member of the youth group. This allowed me to work freely without ever having to worry about innuendo or implications of any impropriety on my part.

In business, this may not be a practical policy, but there are still ways to maintain accountability. I am a big fan of bringing in a neutral "third party" as often as possible, especially when resolving disputes. It cuts down on the "chatter" that almost always follows difficult or heated discussions.

3) Speak positively about others.

This is an interesting one. Why will speaking positively about others instill trust in you? For one thing, it shows people that you have confidence in yourself. If you are willing to build up others, people interpret that as a sign of personal strength; you are not afraid that building others up will somehow diminish you. Those who gossip or berate others in their absence do so, in part, to make themselves look better. For example, if Steve is absent in the Monday morning staff meeting and Jim makes some off-handed comment about Steve having a "long night at the bar" the night before, he is doing so to emphasize the fact that he (Jim) is at work ready to go while Steve is not. In his mind, this makes him look better. In reality this makes him look like someone you should not trust. On the other hand, if Jim sticks up for Steve and throws in a comment about how Steve had been working late over the weekend, the others in the room see that Jim is someone who would stand up for them in their absence. They will make the assumption that Jim is someone whom they can trust to do the right thing.

Chapter 6:

"Imagination"

"Imagination will often carry us to worlds that never were. But without it we go nowhere."

– Carl Sagan

"Where there is no vision, the people perish."

– Proverbs 29:18

One of the key elements in effective leadership is the ability to inspire people through your unique ideas. People aren't looking for leaders who maintain the *status quo*, they are looking for leaders who will take them to new places, show them new things, and create new opportunities for success.

As experts have examined the unprecedented success of Barack Obama and his historic campaign for president, they have all been in agreement on one thing: This man knows how to *inspire* people. His two campaign slogans were, "Yes we can!" and, "Change we can believe in." Both of these were forward-looking and empowering. His platform was not one that encouraged people to sit around waiting for something to happen, it was one that got people up off their couches, into the streets, and into the voting booths.

In order for leaders to inspire people, they must be inspired themselves. What inspires you? What motivates you to be successful? What gets YOU off the couch? A leader must have a big imagination.

As a child I had a lot of interests: dinosaurs, airplanes, space, books, the usual. Like many kids my age, I was very into Legos. The multi-colored blocks came into popularity in the 70s, and I was the perfect age to fully appreciate them. If you don't "get" why Legos are an awesome toy, let me explain. Legos let you build pretty much anything you can imagine. If you want a toy flying car, you can build one with the right pieces. If you want to re-create a key scene from *Star Wars*, you can easily do so. Legos allow children to give physical form to things that previously existed only in their imaginations.

Every Christmas from age eight through twelve, I asked for Legos. I was particularly fond of the "space" Legos, but I was always happy to get them no matter what kind they were or what the particular theme of the set was. Over the years, my brother Barret and I amassed a rather impressive quantity of Legos which we stored in a five-gallon green bucket. When it came time to play with Legos, we would dump the entire bucket out on the floor of our room and begin building. I will never forget the joy of *possibility* that those thousands of plastic pieces represented to me. The pieces were the raw materials from which the ideas in my head would take shape.

Leaders *must* be creative and imaginative, so much so that they are able to create a shared vision in the minds of those whom they lead. Leaders are responsible for coming up with their own ideas and solutions, but perhaps more importantly, they are responsible for inspiring creativity in others. Great leaders give people Legos. Not literally of course, (although that would be cool if they did) but in a figurative sense, leaders help to give people ideas, dreams, visions and then help give those people a means by which they can make them a reality.

In terms of imagination, an effective leader must be able to conceptualize the non-existent. An average leader can see the situation at hand, survey the "battlefield" and make a smart decision, but a *great* leader can see the things that *aren't* there and make a decision based on unseen factors. Great leaders have to be able to see the future and imagine a variety of scenarios. From these imagined scenarios, they develop plans and strategies and base their actions on things that have not yet happened. Imagination is about seeing possibilities.

I learned to play chess at age ten. I've never been that great at it, but I can usually hold my own. I learned how to play from a book that a friend of my mother's gave me for my birthday. At the time, my brother was too young to play, and none of my friends were very interested, so chess started off as a solo activity for me. Chess is a difficult game to play alone, so I was extremely happy later that year when I got a little electronic chess game in which you moved the computer player's pieces to wherever it told you and then you keyed in your own moves. It was cumbersome and took forever to play but that, combined with the book, gave me the opportunity to learn to play chess when there was no one around to teach me. I remember that the computer (which contained a processor much less powerful than the one in the wristwatch I am wearing right now) was very good... at least to a ten-year-old. It was ruthless and decisive, but it taught me the basic rules and even a few unusual strategies which I still employ to this day. I grew to love the game, even though I only beat the computer a handful of times. Chess is a game of forethought. You have to be able to see not only where the pieces are at any given moment, but to *imagine* where they *will be* after your opponent's upcoming moves. Do you know what the following individuals have in common besides being famous and displaying great personal leadership?

- Napoleon Bonaparte
- Marlon Brando
- John Quincy Adams
- Madonna
- Michelle Obama
- Henry Kissinger
- Jimmy Carter
- Winston Churchill
- Bill Cosby
- Queen Elizabeth I
- Frank Sinatra
- David Bowie
- Billy Graham
- Howard Stern
- Al Capone
- Angela Lansbury
- David Letterman
- Joni Mitchell
- Edgar Rice Burroughs

They all are (or were) expert chess players! These all are individuals who had the imagination and forethought to become outstanding in their particular fields by seeing the future before it became the present. They used their imaginations to create a vision and then used their leadership to bring others along on their journeys toward that vision, for better or worse. It's no surprise that they also were good at a game that requires the same sort of skills.

Imagination is not just about seeing the possibilities that the future holds, it is about seeing current situations in a different way. Plenty has been said and written over the past decade about thinking "outside the box," but true leaders ask questions like, "What if there IS no box?" or, "What if the box really isn't a box at all?"

When I was in third grade, I was "fashion-challenged." I insisted on dressing myself, doing my own hair, etc., but the problem was that I almost always chose poorly. When people look back at my school photos from those days, they see a disheveled, disorganized little kid. Even though I enjoyed a certain level of autonomy when it came to my dress, occasionally I would consult my mother. She had worked in clothing and fashion and she was always on top of the latest trends in clothes... *adult* clothes. As I mentioned, however, I was in third grade and not exactly a trend-setter or a model. One Christmas, she bought me an expensive, multicolored rabbit fur coat. She explained to me that it was *très chic* for men to wear fur coats and that I would certainly be the envy of all the other children when I showed up for school sporting such a coat. It made sense to me, so I wore it to class on the first day back after Christmas vacation. As you can imagine, the actual result of wearing the coat was not exactly what I had expected. The children's initial looks of complete incredulity quickly turned to hilarity as I instantly became the funniest thing they had ever seen. The laughter and ridicule continued throughout the day. At recess that afternoon, I thought about leaving the accursed fur in my locker, but it happened to be an unusually cold day so I had no choice but to wear it on the playground. I was a terribly shy child but I also had a bit of a creative spark. I decided that I was going to find a way to redeem the situation in my favor so I grabbed my buddy Sam and hid in the bushes to discuss my predicament. The problem was that the coat looked ridiculous on me but I asked my friend, "What if it really isn't even a coat? What if it is…something else… like a puppet?" Sam agreed that because it was soft and furry it might be able to pass for a puppet so I gave it a shot. I rolled the thing up into a ball, stuck my arm through one of the sleeves, and walked out from behind the bushes. Some kids came over to see what was going on, and I shrewdly explained that I had totally pulled one over on them. My "coat" wasn't merely a coat; it was a very special puppet, as well (sort of like a furry Transformer). I worked the sleeve like it was a nose, made some silly sounds and much to my relief, it worked. They bought it. Soon, more kids gathered around to see my puppet which had somehow made me the "cool" kid on the playground. The embarrassment of the morning disappeared and was replaced by an afternoon of minor celebrity.

I was able to turn around a troubling situation by seeing the rabbit fur coat not for what it was, but for what it *could be*. My imagination saved the day.

As a leader, you have the ability to change the future by imagining what could possibly be. You must be the one who envisions scenarios and solutions which no one around you is able to see. The effectiveness of your leadership will hinge partly on your motivational abilities, but you cannot motivate people unless you first have a concept, an idea, a *vision* to convey to them. In some cases, people won't need much motivation beyond your description of that vision. Think of Dr. Martin Luther King's famous "I Have a Dream" speech. The most memorable part of the speech is when he describes what he *sees:*

"...the day when *all* of God's children, black men and white men, Jews and Gentiles, Protestants and Catholics, will be able to join hands and sing in the words of the old Negro spiritual: 'Free at last! Free at last! Thank God Almighty, we are free at last!'"

That vision began in his imagination. He carefully sculpted the vision, expressed the vision, and set in motion the events that would eventually make those dreams into reality. When people talk about Dr. King, they often describe him as a visionary. The dictionary defines the word as such:

VISIONARY- *noun*

1) A person of unusually keen foresight.

2) A person who sees visions.

3) A person who is given to audacious, highly speculative, or impractical ideas or schemes; dreamer.

Pay particular attention to the third definition. If you are a leader, get used to hearing people describe your ideas as "audacious" or "impractical." In 1963, when Dr. King delivered the legendary message, many people used those same words to describe his vision of the future. In 1963, "integration" was a volatile word. Black children were being kept out of public schools by force. In January 2009, Barack Obama became the first black President of the United States. Progress starts with vision. Vision starts with imagination.

In my own experience as a leader, I have found that keeping my imagination flowing has often been a significant challenge. Occasionally I just run out of ideas or the ideas that I do have just seem tired and trite. There are always problems to be solved, but sometimes I just can't think of a suitably creative answer. When this happens, there are a few things I have learned to do to get my imagination moving when it seems to be stalled:

1) Read.

When my own thoughts begin to bore me or when the ideas in my head don't sufficiently inspire me, I often turn to the words of others for inspiration. Through books I keep a fresh stream of ideas flowing into my mind to nourish and water the seeds of my imagination. As a professional speaker by trade, I occasionally read books by other "inspirational speakers" to see what they have to say and to help kick-start my creativity. I am not looking to take other people's concepts and somehow rework them as my own, I am looking for thoughts and ideas which will cause something to stir in my *own* imagination. I also tend to read several books at a time, each representing a completely different literary genre. This creates a broader pallet from which to establish my own ideas. For example, I recently finished the book *Slash*, the autobiography of the legendary Guns N' Roses guitarist. Slash is certainly no Tony Robbins, but I love his music. As I read the book, I marveled at how such a deeply troubled and damaged man could create such influential and (dare I say?) inspiring music. It got me thinking about words like "influence," "passion," and "integrity." These words spawned streams of thought which quite literally led me to several ideas in the book you are reading.

2) Watch.

Few things are as inspiring as watching a master craftsman at work. Whatever you most enjoy doing, find someone who is a master at that particular activity and watch them do it. If you are an athlete, watch some highlight reels of your favorite basketball, football, or baseball player. If you are a musician, watch a concert (in person if you can) by your favorite band. If you are a minister, watch a sermon by a preacher who moves you.

For the last six years, I have had the honor of being a speaker and presenter for Monster.com's "Making it Count" programs. These programs encourage students to strive for success in a variety of arenas including their academic studies and in their college searches. Each semester I have the opportunity to train with some of the best speakers in the country. For me, the highlights of every training weekend are the times when I can just sit back and watch some truly amazing speakers do what they were born to do. I always leave inspired and full of new ideas for the semester ahead.

3) Be healthy.

It is a scientific fact that your mind works better when your body is healthy, and the way to keep your body healthy is through proper diet and exercise. There are no magic pills or formulas to make you healthy… you *must* eat right and you *must* exercise. Not only do I agree with this concept in theory, but I have seen it work for me personally. The whole concept of "Inertia" as it relates to leadership and the I.N.E.R.T.I.A. acronym came to me during several days of intense exercise which followed a long period of "writer's block." When you exercise, your body releases certain neurotransmitters that can actually generate *new neurons* in your brain! Conversely, the chemicals, preservatives, and saturated fats in unhealthy foods have been shown to negatively affect brain chemistry. Some scientists have even shown a direct link between unhealthy eating and clinical depression.

Chapter 7:

"Authenticity"

"...we long for that most elusive quality in our leaders— the quality of authenticity, of being who you say you are, of possessing a truthfulness that goes beyond words."

-President Barack Obama

In 2003 a friend gave me a book that he said had "changed his life." It was a memoir about a man's recovery from drug and alcohol addiction called *A Million Little Pieces*. I took the book home and read it in less than a week. The material was graphic, intensely disturbing, and absolutely moving. It also happened to be fictional.

The author James Frey received critical and popular acclaim for the book upon its release due largely to the endorsement and attention it got from Oprah Winfrey. Millions of people bought and read the book and many, like my friend, reported that the book was so challenging and inspirational that it had, indeed, changed their lives. Once the truth came out, Oprah had Frey on her show to apologize for misleading the public, but the damage was done. The amount of betrayal and anger Frey's readers expressed was unprecedented— but why? Why were people so upset when they found out that the events chronicled in the book didn't happen the way Frey portrayed them as having happened? Because people value authenticity. They want the real deal and when they find out that what they have is not the real deal, the disappointment cuts deeply.

I suppose there was a time when leaders were able to maintain a public persona as well as a private one but these days, as I mentioned before, when you step out into the spotlight as a leader, you must be prepared to lose a big part of your private life. People want legitimacy and authenticity in their leaders. When they begin to sense that a leader is saying one thing while doing another, they will turn against that leader very quickly. In today's world, particularly in the US, leaders must be willing to be authentic. When it comes down to it, it is really an issue of character. A woman of character has no problem being authentic because she has nothing to hide. The public has embraced this idea and will not accept anything less from their leaders.

People ask me all the time why I left the church world and the ministry after almost twelve years of service. Although there are a number of reasons, I think this idea of authenticity factored greatly into my decision to leave. Over the years, people change. Their ideas and opinions evolve and their policies as leaders reflect these changes. In the church world, in general, I found there to be very little room for personal evolution. During the last few years of my service at Harbor Point, I underwent a lot of personal and spiritual changes. I realized that many of the things I had held true for most of my life were, in fact, not true, or at least, not as true as I had been told. My theology started to veer a bit to the left while the church itself remained entrenched in fundamentalist, evangelical ideology. At this point, I realized I could do one of three things. I could stay and pretend everything was ok and that I still completely agreed with the church's policies, I could fight the uphill battle of trying to change the thinking of several thousand people in the church, or I could leave to pursue a different career. I chose the third option and I haven't looked back.

If I had stayed and continued to allow people to believe that my views on key issues remained steadfast, I would have been dishonest not just to them but to myself as well. I could not bear the idea of not being authentic with the congregation I was serving. I knew that they deserved authenticity in their leadership and that at the time, I was not able to provide that.

Authenticity goes hand-in-hand with trust. When people believe in leaders, they are giving them a great deal of trust and they are believing that their leaders are being authentic in return. A lack of authenticity is a betrayal of trust.

One of the most authentic leaders I have ever known is a man named Mark Cuban. If you follow sports, you no doubt know him as the billionaire owner of the Dallas Mavericks basketball team. In 1996 however, he was merely the millionaire Mark Cuban, owner of a small internet startup company called AudioNet. While in college, several years before, Cuban had dreamed of a day in which he could somehow listen to his favorite college sports broadcasts *anywhere*, even if he was nowhere near the areas in which the games were being broadcast. With the advent of the Internet and its explosion in popularity in the early nineties, his vision became a reality. In 1996, AudioNet became the Internet's first major broadcasting company. The website "streamed" audio from hundreds of different radio stations and recorded sources all over the world to anyone with a computer and a modem. For the first time, distance from the broadcast source became irrelevant. Today, we take this sort of thing for granted but it 1996, it was a pretty big deal. I went to work for AudioNet shortly after I graduated from college. At the time, my job was to acquire audio content for the website and to act as something of a *liaison* to the content providers, mostly audiobook companies and small record labels. The work was fun and interesting but in retrospect, one of the most valuable things I gained from the job was exposure to Mark Cuban and his unique leadership style. These days, when I talk to people about Mark, I always tell them that he is one of the most authentic people I have ever met. The Mark you see on TV or in the media is the Mark you get when you are sitting in his office or talking to him on the street. He is just as animated, blunt, humorous, and manic as he is courtside when he is yelling obscenities at officials and opposing players. (So far he has accrued at least $1,665,000 in NBA fines for 13 incidents.)

I remember once during the AudioNet days, Mark was scheduled to attend a very important meeting with some high-profile executives from some big companies who were considering purchasing AudioNet. The men all showed up for the meeting in their thousand-dollar suits, sporting pricey briefcases and laptops, and Mark walked into the meeting wearing jeans, a sweatshirt, and Top-Sider shoes with no socks. One of the executives at the meeting had heard of Cuban's penchant for sockless footwear and actually brought him a pair of socks as a joke. Mark, of course, accepted the gift but explained that he was perfectly comfortable the way he was.

It was not surprising to me at all when it was eventually announced that Mark and his partner Todd Wagner had sold the company to Yahoo! for $5.9 billion. Likewise, it wasn't the least bit surprising later when Mark made his way into the *Guinness Book of Records* in 1999 by making the "largest single e-commerce transaction," the purchase of a $40 million Gulfstream V jet, the plane he flies in to attend Mavericks games when they are on the road. He does exactly what he wants to do and seems to care very little about public opinion of him or his methods. This is part of what makes him such a great leader. The people on his team and in his various organizations always know that they are getting the real deal. You can say a lot of things about Mark, but one thing you can't say about him, is that he is not authentic.

If you have ever been to Italy, chances are you have been to Florence. If you have been to Florence, chances are you have seen Michelangelo's statue of David. It is possibly the most famous statue ever created. As I mentioned previously in the book, I spent a lot of time in Italy a few years ago and while I was there I had the opportunity to visit Florence and to see the statue. I was unprepared for how amazing the actual statue is when you view it in person. It is much bigger than you would imagine and it is absolutely *flawless*. For me, it was almost unfathomable that a human being could produce such a perfect image from a piece of marble. The lines, the muscles, the face, the eyes... everything about David is breathtakingly perfect.

In pretty much any famous city in the world, you can find on every corner numerous replicas of the city's noted landmarks, buildings, or works of art. In New York, you can buy a Statue of Liberty at any corner store. In Paris, you can purchase your very own Eiffel Tower for the cost of a cup of coffee. In Florence, the statue of David is everywhere. On the day I saw the statue at the Gallery of the *Accademia di Belle Arti* I toured the rest of the city as well. I visited a scenic overlook near the river from which you can see a good portion of the city. I remember seeing a full-sized bronze replica of Michelangelo's statue at the overlook and feeling... sad...under-whelmed. Although it was an "exact" replica of the masterpiece, it was dirty, greenish and covered with pigeons. Even though the shape was essentially the same, the *soul* was missing. There is something magical in the authentic work that can never be duplicated. There really is no substitute for authenticity.

I grew up in a less-than-affluent family situation. My mother struggled to make ends meet and to raise my brother, my sister, and myself on an extremely tight budget. She taught me the value of money and how to cut corners at the store when you have to. As kids, it was a rare treat when we were able to buy "name brand" products rather than the discounted generic versions. Over the years, however, I have become somewhat obsessed with authenticity. When I go to the grocery store, I buy real butter, not margarine. I like real coffee, not decaf. I don't like "reduced-fat," "low-sodium," or "light" *anything!* Give me the real thing every time. When it comes to people, I prefer to spend my time with people who have an air of authenticity about them as well, even if they are not like me in any way. As a leader, you will attract a loyal following when you convey authenticity in your voice, body language and actions. People these days, especially young people, are keenly aware of leaders who put on airs or attempt to appear cool or knowledgeable when they are neither. They will scan you very quickly and if they decide that you are anything less than authentic, they will write you off in a hurry and you will instantly diminish your effectiveness as a leader.

Your authenticity will serve you well. When people learn that you have *substance* rather than just style and when they realize that you are willing to stand behind your ideas and opinions despite outside pressure to change them, they will embrace you and will follow you with an amazing amount of loyalty. When people believe that you are real, they will extend that same belief to your leadership. Strive for complete authenticity in your leadership style. Here are three keys to maintaining authenticity in your leadership:

1) Value yourself, your ideas, and your unique style.

Many leaders make the mistake of trying too hard to be liked by others. They have this image in their mind of what the people want, and they try to mold themselves into that image. The problem with this is that people can see right through this ruse. In the "open" age we live in, it is very difficult to fool people. A strong leader knows that who they already are is good enough and valuable enough without having to try to be someone else. Learn to appreciate the unique qualities of other people without trying to emulate them or copy the things that work for them. Those things may not necessarily work for you, and in fact, they may do you more harm than good. Be who you are and people will be drawn to you.

2) Watch yourself.

The next time you give a speech, deliver a presentation, or run a meeting, record yourself doing it and watch the recording at a later time. Look at yourself from an "outsider's" point-of-view, with an objective, critical eye. Pretend that you are one of the people in the audience. Do you come across as authentic? Do you look like you are "trying too hard?" This is a very challenging thing to do and actually, I really don't like doing it myself. However, I have found that it is an amazingly effective way to judge your own authenticity.

Take notes on what you did well and what you can improve upon and then actually practice in front of a mirror. It will be uncomfortable at first, but it will teach you to settle down and be real with your audience. Speaking of settling down...

3) Relax.

I've seen many great leaders give a lot of great speeches but what I've seen more often is *potentially* great leaders *trying* to give great speeches. A few weeks ago, I was delivering a presentation to a group of seasoned, veteran professional speakers. I didn't feel like I knew the material as well as I should have and I was more than nervous. (Speaking in front of a thousand teenagers is infinitely easier than speaking in front of a small room of professional speakers, trust me.) After lunch on the day of my presentation, I went to my hotel room and tried to run through the material out loud. I stumbled and fumbled and completely blanked out! It was horrifying. I found myself at a complete loss. I felt like I was going to blow the speech big time. Eventually, I realized that I was running out of time and getting nowhere with my practicing. I dialed up some calm meditation music on my computer, changed into some shorts and a T-shirt, put a pillow on the floor and sat down in a yoga "lotus" position. As I looked out the window at the setting sun, I became conscious of my breathing. It was quick and choppy so I slowed it down. In through the nose... out through the mouth. Over the next twenty minutes, I just sat there. I didn't think about my speech, I didn't think about the stress, I didn't think about *anything*. I just relaxed and breathed. When it came time to go, I bounced up, got dressed and hurried down to the meeting room. That afternoon, I ended up delivering a near-flawless speech. I remembered all the parts I had forgotten and my *real* self came out in the presentation. I was able to be authentic once I relaxed.

Chapter 8

Putting it All Together...

Most people who know me know that my favorite musical group of all time is the Irish band U2. I own all sixteen of their official albums as well as many "bootlegs," imports, and live records. I have been a fan since around 1986 and consider them to be one of the most important groups in the history of rock music. If you aren't familiar with the greatness that is U2, here are the facts you should know:

-Formed in Dublin, Ireland, in 1976

-All original members of the band, singer Paul David Hewson (known as Bono), guitarist David Howell Evans (known as The Edge,) bassist Adam Clayton, and drummer Larry Mullen, Jr., have been with the band since its inception.

-Sold over 140 million albums worldwide

- Won 22 Grammys (the most by any band)

- Inducted in 2005 into the Rock and Roll Hall of Fame (in their first year of eligibility)

- Listed by *Rolling Stone* magazine as #22 in their list of the greatest artists of all time

I was listening to the song "With or Without You" today as I was thinking about how to end this book. I decided that I needed to talk about a leader who summed up all seven of the INERTIA principles in one package and to me, that leader is Bono. In closing, please allow me to recap the seven principles and to explain how Bono exemplifies each one to me...

INTENT

Although Bono co-founded U2 in 1976 with the other members, he quickly established himself as the leader of the band. He started off writing nearly all of the music and lyrics and continues to do so today. In 1986, as the band was beginning to gain notoriety, he explained to *Rolling Stone* that not only was he interested in music but in becoming involved in various social and political causes as well. Today he actively involves himself in organizations such as Amnesty International and DATA (Debt, AIDS, Trade, Africa), and aggressively campaigns for a variety of human rights causes and social justice efforts. In 2006, Tom Zeller of *The New York Times* described Bono as "the face of fusion philanthropy." Although he could not have possibly known in 1976 how big his band would become, he had the *intent* to lead from the very beginning.

NECESSITY

Obviously, when U2 began, there was a necessity for a lead singer and songwriter. Bono saw the opportunity to join the band when he saw Larry Mullen, Jr.'s, posting on his secondary school's bulletin board and he jumped into the role headfirst. However, in the early eighties, it had not yet become fashionable for musicians to overtly support socio-political causes. There was a need for leadership from the rock community and Bono stepped in. Over the years, Bono has personally overseen movements and campaigns such as the *Jubilee 2000* project which focused on debt-relief for impoverished nations. Bono has never had to force himself into leadership roles because his passion and availability have made him a natural fit for the jobs when there was a leadership vacuum.

ENERGY

It takes a lot of positive energy to keep a band together for more than thirty years. While many other superstar groups have come and gone over the years, typically succumbing to the trappings of "sex, drugs, and rock 'n roll" excesses, Bono and U2 have managed to not only stay together, but to stay *relevant*. People are drawn to Bono's songs, not just because of their musical accessibility, but because of their enduring message of hope in the face of human struggle. When you see Bono in public, he smiles a lot, he jokes with people (even with world leaders like presidents Bill Clinton and George W. Bush,) and he shares his vision for a better world. In total, I've probably seen at least two hundred U2 performances over the years on television, in videos, on film, and live in concert, and I can truly say that they *always* put on a good show. They bring an element of passion and energy to the stage that few bands can match, especially almost thirty years into their career.

RESILIENCE

The rock and roll industry is a notoriously mean business. Bands come and go on an almost daily basis and when a band falls out of favor with the public, they are rarely able to revive their careers. U2 has never really had to worry about this problem though because ALL of their albums have been commercially, critically, and fiscally successful. When popular trends in music lean toward very particular genres, U2's resilience and flexibility allows them to tweak their sound and weave their way through the trends. They have not only survived the musical upheavals of the past three decades (New Wave, Heavy Metal, Rap, Grunge, Techno, etc.) but they have thrived *despite* them.

TRUST

In Bob Dylan's classic 1967 song "All Along the Watchtower" he claimed that all he had was "…a red guitar, three chords, and the truth." In 1988, U2 covered the song on its *Rattle and Hum* film and record. When Bono sang that famous line, people *believed* him… they trusted that he was speaking "the truth." The word "trustworthy" does not often come to mind when describing rock stars but U2 fans genuinely trust Bono. Throughout his long career, he has almost completely avoided public scandals and has, by all accounts, been faithful to his wife Alison Hewson. He has established a reputation as a respectable and thoughtful individual… the kind of guy people just innately trust.

IMAGINATION

Have you ever actually sat down and written a song? Even though I have been a musician since I was sixteen and have played in a number of bands, I have found songwriting to be one of the most creatively challenging things one can do. I'd say that over the years I've written probably a dozen or so songs, VERY few of which were any good. Bono has written almost *six hundred songs*, dozens of which were legitimate hit tunes. As I said in chapter six, imagination is about being able to see things that are not there. It takes a pretty developed imagination to write a song, but it takes an *amazing* amount of imagination to write six hundred of them. To create a musical idea in your head, and then to follow it through all the way to the recording stage is an impressive feat. To do it as well and as often as Bono has is genuinely amazing.

AUTHENTICITY

When people ask me to name one celebrity I think would be cool to sit down and have a beer with, Bono is always the first name that comes to mind. There are plenty of artists, actors, politicians, and writers whom I admire and would like to meet, but Bono seems like the kind of person who would answer my questions honestly, not like a star. The causes that Bono has championed over the years are not self-serving causes, they are causes that have benefited poor children in Africa and AIDS victims in Latin America. These are not people who will be purchasing U2 records. Bono has a genuine and authentic interest in helping people and his actions have always backed up his words.

Whether you are the CEO of a Fortune 500 company, or the manager of a small pizza restaurant in Omaha, you *can* become a better leader. Regardless of your level of success or leadership experience, you can always make improvements that will allow you the opportunity to influence more people in a stronger way. Your job as a leader is to take your people to a new place... to infuse them with the energy that creates motion. It all comes back to physics. According to the laws of inertia, objects that are at rest will stay at rest until something, or some*one* moves them. Are you ready to be that someone? Are you ready to be an intentional leader, seeking out those opportunities and stepping boldly into position? Are you ready to harness your own positive energy so that it will be transferred to those around you? If you truly desire to become an effective, successful leader, it is time for you to earn the trust of others and establish an authentic reputation. Explore the depths of your creative imagination. Be authentic. Be yourself. Go out and change the world! Godspeed.

About the Author:

Brandon Walker is a professional speaker and trainer specializing in leadership development and personal health and fitness.

Based out of Dallas, TX, Brandon travels full-time presenting dynamic seminars on a variety of topics. His five "flagship" programs include:

- "Inside Out: Three Dimensional Leadership"
- "Road Well: Health and Fitness for the Business Traveler"
- "Off the Couch: The Kid's Fitness Guide for Parents!"
- "High School 101: The Parent's Guide to Student Success"
- "God is Green: Reconciling Religion and Environmental Responsibility"

For booking and further information please visit:

www.brandonwalker.org

214-763-0614 / brandon@brandonwalker.org

Made in the USA
Lexington, KY
06 October 2010